"All over this nation, God is stirring the hearts of men to rise up and enter into their God-given destiny. Lou Turner's lifelong passion is to see men enter into their divine purpose in life. 'Living Life God's Way,' of which this book is a part, is born out of this passion. Throughout this Bible study series, Turner opens up God's Word to help you discover HIS plan for your success in your life, family, and work. If you are ready to get off the treadmill, to begin to enjoy God's fullness in your life and make a significant contribution to the world around you, I recommend that you dive into this life-transforming Bible study."

Hal H. Sacks, D.Min., *BridgeBuilders International Leadership Network*

"It seems North American culture is rapidly moving toward what the Bible calls 'everyone doing what is right in his own mind' (Judges 21:25). The prophet Isaiah declared, 'Woe to those who call evil, good, and good, evil' (Isaiah 5:20). This Bible study series will challenge every man in the 21st century as 'iron sharpens iron'! The Q&As at the end of each chapter really personalize the teaching."

Dennis Conner, *Co-Founder/President, Called to Serve Prayer-Coaching Ministry*

"I have known Lou Turner for over twenty years. Lou loves Jesus and has built his life on the Word of God. Lou's Bible study series, 'Living Life God's Way,' is full of biblical truth that has been tested and can be applied by disciples of Jesus in practical ways. These books will help you grow in your faith and gain confidence and competence, which will increase your fruitfulness in Christ.

Mark Buckley, *Founding Pastor of Living Streams Church*

Living Life God's Way

The Test of Pride

Lou Turner

The Test of Pride
First Edition, 2020
Copyright © 2020 by Lou Turner

The Test of Pride is part of the Living Life God's Way Series by Lou Turner.

All rights reserved. No part of this publication may be reproduced, stored in a retrieval system, or transmitted in any form by any means—electronic, mechanical, photocopy, recording, or otherwise—except for brief quotations in critical reviews or articles, without the prior permission of the publisher, except as provided by U.S. copyright law.

Unless otherwise identified, Scripture quotations are from the ESV® Bible (The Holy Bible, English Standard Version®), copyright © 2001 by Crossway, a publishing ministry of Good News Publishers. Used by permission. All rights reserved.

Scripture quotations marked (NIV) are taken from the Holy Bible, New International Version®, NIV®. Copyright © 1973, 1978, 1984, 2011 by Biblica, Inc.™ Used by permission of Zondervan. All rights reserved worldwide. www.zondervan.com. The "NIV" and "New International Version" are trademarks registered in the United States Patent and Trademark Office by Biblica, Inc.

Some of the anecdotal illustrations in this book are true to life and are included with the permission of the persons involved. All other illustrations are composites of real situations, and any resemblance to people living or dead is coincidental.

To order additional books:
www.amazon.com
www.hislifeinus.com

ISBN: 978-1-7331186-8-2

Editorial and Book Packaging: Inspira Literary Solutions, Gig Harbor, WA
Book Design: PerfecType, Nashville, TN
Cover Design: MTWdesign, Dickson, TN
Printed in the USA by Ingram Spark

He will be like a tree firmly planted by streams of water,
Which yields its fruit in its season
And its leaf does not wither;
And in whatever he does, he prospers.

Psalm 1:3

TABLE OF CONTENTS

Preface ix

How to Use this Book xi

Introduction xiii

Pride versus Humility 1

Breaking Free of Blind Spots 15

Living in True Humility 25

A Final Word 37

About the Author 39

PREFACE

We live in a world that has largely forgotten what manhood is about. In the Western world, men are often portrayed on television as buffoons who are out of touch and must rely on their wives to straighten them out. These characters are portrayed as silly, insensitive, lacking common sense, and when they do speak, they are generally wrong. They are generally portrayed as either ridiculously weak or overly macho. They are not able to commit to a long-term relationship and generally mistreat women. Positive role models are hard to find in the media.

However, the Bible teaches a different type of manhood, the authentic one. Men are to be leaders, loving their wives and children, excelling in their work, and standing for truth. They are to be men of wisdom, knowledge, having godly character and seeking after God and His direction. They are to be exhibiting godly leadership at church, in the community, and in business, and to be a light to those around them. They are to be men of compassion and love, as well as courageous and bold when needed.

Men go astray from these ideals, including Christian men, due to improper convictions or beliefs about life. They have received these from various sources: well-meaning family and friends, the media, and the culture around them—a world system that promotes the tearing down of God's biblical truths.

PREFACE

But without proper biblical foundation, we will all go astray. That's why I wrote these books, containing insights, observations, and biblical truths distilled over the course of my decades of life and ministry. Each section is designed to be a stand-alone section for study and consideration. I hope this series, *Living Life God's Way*, will be used to disciple men in biblical truths for life. Whether you use it for yourself, with a group, or to mentor or disciple someone else, my hope is that it will be a blessing to you and encourage you to seek God and grow in Him.

HOW TO USE THIS BOOK

What does it mean to be a "good" husband and father?
How do I live out the Christian life at work?
What does God want from me—and how am I supposed to find that out?

These were questions that plagued me as a young man—questions, I learned, that are at the front of many men's minds at various times in their lives. For me, these questions began my quest to seek God and discover the answers, and my discoveries, over the years of my life, led to this series of booklets, *Living Life God's Way*. The series discusses 13 topics that every man must deal with, regardless of his work, calling, profession, or circumstances. It is difficult to know how to live the Christian life without understanding what God says about these areas of life.

These topics are:

1. Seeking and Finding God
2. Who You Are in Christ
3. A Man's Work and Ministry
4. Understanding Authority
5. A Man and His Wife
6. A Man and His Children
7. Getting God's Guidance and Direction

8. Overcoming Strongholds
9. A Man and Money
10. Repentance, Forgiveness, and Restitution
11. Being a Leader
12. A Man and Sex
13. The Test of Pride

You can use these books to study on your own, in a small group, or with a larger group of men. Each topic or booklet is a stand-alone study, and a person can begin with any one he chooses. They are different lengths and can be adapted to various settings—home, church, or community—all topics that are pertinent to today.

Explore what the Bible says about these important and critical areas. The encouragement is to read these with an open heart, asking God to reveal His truth to you in each of these areas of life. Pray that His Spirit will show you His truth, so that you may live in it and enjoy all God has for you. I pray that you experience the blessing and presence of God in your life as you draw closer to Him and more aware of His leading in every area of your life.

INTRODUCTION TO A TEST OF PRIDE

Many people may not realize the importance of the topic of pride and humility. But it is of great importance for all. The path our lives take, whether greatly blessed or filled with difficulty, may be determined by whether or not pride is an issue for us. This one issue can result in hardships and trials coming our way in order for God to teach us humility.

While life will inevitably have hardships and trials, the ones brought on by pride can be especially difficult, until we understand what God is trying to do in our lives .

Pride not only affects a man and his relationship with God; it also affects his relationships with his wife, his children, and others around him. Our pride can hurt those closest to us. Pride can also greatly diminish our usefulness to God and our effectiveness in His Kingdom. It can even lead to our falling away from the faith. That makes it crucial for us to consider the important topic of pride seriously and prayerfully.

Chapter 1

Pride versus Humility

I want to begin by confessing I am still learning in this area. I have learned much, but am continuing to learn about what I will be sharing in this book. I admit that I do not have it all together (I never will). But I would like to share things I have learned. With that said, let's jump into this important topic.

Years ago, I was at a week-long workshop with a group of men. My company, a large international firm, had sent a number of its management team there. Though we participants didn't know it beforehand, one of the purposes of the training was to expose strengths and weaknesses of the participants so we could become more effective managers. I had never been to anything like this and was enjoying the open candor and interaction.

On the last evening, the team of six I had been a part of all week was to evaluate each team member, listing strengths and weaknesses. Those being evaluated could say nothing until it was over. Each evaluation lasted anywhere from 45 minutes to 90 minutes.

When it was my turn to be evaluated, while the men mentioned some strengths, one of the focus points they agreed on was that pride was a problem in my life. One man said, "Thinks he knows it all." Another said, "He has a holier-than-thou attitude." It was hard to hear, but as I listened, I realized they were right.

At the end, when I was allowed to speak, all I could do was apologize for my prideful attitudes and tell them that it was my purpose to work on it so it would not be such a weakness in my life. I realized it was a problem with the men in that room, many who had only known me for that week. But I also realized my pride had to be a problem for others in my life. Others had been trying to tell me about this problem, but it had not struck home like it did that evening.

I was humbled, and also became motivated to seek God about this area and ask Him to change me. As I prayed about it over time, the Lord began to give me insight about how pride had affected my relationships with my wife, my friends, people in my church, and people in my business life. But more importantly, I began to see how it had affected my relationship with God.

I realized I had bought into the world system's concept of being totally self-reliant. I liked to be right and wanted others to always think I was right. I tried not to show weakness or admit I was wrong. In fact, it was difficult for me to *ever* admit I was wrong!

I also came to realize that because I was insecure, I felt I had to show others I was right about things to build myself up. I really needed to discover God's love for me, that my acceptance and security were in my relationship with Him, not in myself.

I wish pride were a "one-and-done" area for me—that I could deal it with once and for all and be done with it. But my journey in life has come up against this area more than once. I imagine that's true for many of us.

Pride can have a great, negative affect our lives. While there is a positive area of pride, most of us struggle with the negative side. Destructive pride is the type defined as "an unduly high opinion of oneself; exaggerated self-esteem; conceit and the haughty behavior resulting from arrogance; thinking of yourself as better than others." In this study, we are dealing with the kind of destructive pride warned about in the Bible:

"When pride comes, then comes shame; but with the humble is wisdom" (Proverbs 11:2).

"Pride goes before destruction, and a haughty spirit before a fall. Better to be of a humble spirit with the lowly, than to divide the spoil with the proud" (Proverbs 16:18-19).

"A man's pride will bring him low, but the humble in spirit will retain honor" (Proverbs 29:23).

"The fear of the LORD is to hate evil; pride and arrogance and the evil way and the perverse mouth I hate" (Proverbs 8:13).

*"Everyone who is proud in heart is an **abomination** to the LORD; though they join forces, none will go unpunished" (Proverbs 16:5, emphasis added).*

Proverbs is a great book in the Bible. It tells it like it is. These are short, clear, easy-to-understand statements. They are God-spoken truths, and we are well advised to heed them. It is evident from these scriptures that God is opposed to pride. More than that, these scriptures indicate that a proud person will suffer consequences in life because of his or her pride. Let's take a closer look and see what we can discover about pride.

The Prideful Man

One of the issues with a proud man is that he thinks of himself as better than others. A proud person wants to be exalted for his accomplishments, and usually wants to be in authority. He believes he is the one best suited to be in control of the situation. If you think you are always right, then you should lead. Right?

It is difficult for a proud person to step back and let others lead, or to want to serve others. A proud person wants others to admire and serve him. He does not give credit to God for all he has and does not have a proper attitude of gratitude and thanksgiving for God's blessings. He usually wants to take credit for the good things that happen in his life. After all, he made it happen, right? Not according to Scripture.

The prideful person believes he always knows best and has little or no need for guidance or help from others. He is not very open to correction or advice, and finds it difficult to accept when offered. The prideful person has exaggerated self-esteem that leads to arrogance. He sees himself as his greatest resource, rather than his relationship with God.

If he is a spiritually motivated man, then he is probably spiritually proud, thinking he knows best and His relationship with God is better than others. He wants to be exalted, lifted up, and recognized as an exceptional person. Since he believes he is usually right, he wants to be in control of everything around him. He may feel no real need of God. Or, he may acknowledge God with his lips, but his heart is the problem. In his heart he is a proud man, in the negative sense.

What might that look like as it plays out in one's life? Let's look at some of the ways pride may display itself:

The prideful man:

- finds it difficult to acknowledge his failures and shortcomings, and sees no need for forgiveness
- does not freely submit to God or His truth as revealed in the Bible
- sees no need for his heart and mind to be changed in order to agree with God. He considers himself to be okay—or close to perfect
- does not understand his need for God's grace; his "works" earn what he needs
- often condemns or is overly critical of others
- puts his own needs first
- believes in himself as the one he should rely on
- is caught up in his goals, aspirations, and desires—and everyone must fit into his direction

Sinful pride reveals itself by the motivation of the heart. Pride exalts itself and causes a person to exalt himself. Since a proud person exalts himself, he seeks to promote himself and craves recognition and approval. Pride causes a hunger that needs to be fed: the ego. This need often comes from a deep need to be accepted or from a sense of inferiority. How much better to be accepted than to be exalted and admired! Often a man who wants to be admired and sees his sense of worth coming from being better than others, or from always being right or "in the know," will revel in his accomplishments and feel insecure when he is not standing out in some way.

He may be driven and will have a need to be lifted up, or will lift himself up when around others. He can't be average; in fact, he may feel that being average admits defeat. Or, if he does not have a drive to show others up, he may content himself in thinking others are always wrong and he is right. Intimate relationships may be difficult. I'm not talking about sexual intimacy, but intimacy where you are not able to share your soul or heart with others for fear of being exposed, or for fear of others discovering you are less than perfect after all. We can have this fear whether or not we have a problem with pride. But a proud person guards his persona constantly in order to keep up his image. It's usually all about him.

Pride may surface in a number of these ways in different degrees. A person with a pride problem may not show all of these traits, but a number of them.

The Humble Man

The alternative to pride is humility. Humility is recognizing that all we have is from God. Noah Webster's 1828 Dictionary defines humility as "freedom from pride and arrogance, humbleness of mind, a deep sense of one's own unworthiness of God's goodness, but thankful for it." A humble person knows in his heart that all he has that is good is from God and wants to honor Him for it.

The humble Christian recognizes that, on his own without God, he would go astray. The humble man knows that, left to himself, he could make self-centered choices that would be harmful to his life. He has a holy distrust of being only self reliant, of trusting only in himself, and he recognizes his need of God.

Many men who have considered themselves to be of average ability have been very successful. They have given the credit to God's blessing on their life, not to their own abilities. Yes, they may have worked hard and given it their best. But so have many others and have not succeeded. They realize God has blessed their efforts. This is what it means to operate in humility. The humble man:

- recognizes his failures and shortcomings and is grateful for God's love and forgiveness
- submits to God and His truth as revealed in His Word, the Bible
- realizes his heart and mind needs to be changed and renewed in order to agree with God
- recognizes and accepts God's grace and is thankful for it
- does not condemn or become overly critical of himself or others
- when appropriate, puts others' needs before his own
- desires to submit to God's leadership and guidance because he understands he has an inherent need to do so
- seeks God for direction in life and yields to His Lordship and direction, trusting that God will lead him into what is best for his life

Humility allows a man to step back and let others lead, when appropriate. He is willing to follow Jesus in humbly serving others. He listens to advice and correction, and lets God use others to speak truth to him and desires God to change him as needed.

The humble man sees himself honestly, with no need to exalt himself in arrogance to prove who he is. This does not mean a man who is motivated to lead will not do so, but he is able to support others when they lead.

To have a strong drive and desire to succeed is not wrong. Giving yourself the credit and promoting yourself as the one who made it all happen is where pride enters in.

In truth, all of us struggle at times with pride. That does not mean we are ego-maniacs, but that part of our journey is to become more trusting and reliant on God, and less trusting of ourselves without His guidance. It doesn't mean we should not desire to accomplish all we can, but that we trust and rely on God's guidance and direction. We all have to "guard our hearts," so that our motivation is not prideful; to lift ourselves up as being better than others or not needing God.

A person can be motivated to succeed in his work, take a positive pride in doing quality work, and have a strong personality. But if he has a sense of humility, he gives praise and credit to God for blessing his efforts, opening doors of opportunity for him, and helping him in all he does. We all need to seek the Lord for His leadership in our life. It can be harder for highly motivated people to humble themselves before the Lord and seek His leadership. But as God works in our life, this can happen—for any of us.

God Teaches a King Humility

God is committed to conforming us to the image and character of His Son, and to remove those things in our lives, such as pride, that hurt us or hold us back. He uses various methods to get our attention and motivate us to seek Him for wisdom and direction with an open heart. For example, when God decides to deal with a man's pride or self reliance, his work may begin to fall apart, or he may begin to experience adversity in some area of life (though adversity does not always mean God is dealing with pride).

Our loving Father does not take pleasure in seeing His child go through adversity.

He does take pleasure in seeeing the character of Christ being formed in us. During adversity, we usually are more open to hearing from God and really listening to what He is saying to us. In these times, God can speak to us and often more readily change us into the person He desires us to be. He wants us to have a more meaningful relationship with Him and others so He can use us in a greater way. He may use adversity to strengthen us and build character.

PRIDE VERSUS HUMILITY

The story of Nebuchadnezzar in Daniel 4 is a poignant example of this, and of the tragic results of pride. Nebuchadnezzar was possibly the most powerful king on the earth at the time. His great power, his victories, and his accomplishments were from the Lord. In fact, the Bible says that God used Nebuchadnezzar as His instrument to exact judgment on other nations, whether he realized it or not (see Jeremiah 27:4-8).

However, Nebuchadnezzar began to take the credit for all he had acquired and accomplished. He said in his heart that he, in his own strength, might, talent, and abilities, had done all of the great deeds and created his empire. He had a real problem with pride.

Daniel, a prophet of God who served Nebuchadnezzar, warned the king that if he did not turn from his pride and give God the glory, God would humble him in a dramatic way. However, Nebuchadnezzar was unwilling to heed Daniel's warning. The king paid the price for his pride (please read his story in Daniel chapter 4).

God humbled Nebuchadnezzar by causing him to lose his sanity and live like an animal in the fields for a time. When he came to his senses, he humbled himself before God and repented of his pride. He sent a letter to all his peoples describing his repentance:

> *But at the end of that period, I, Nebuchadnezzar, raised my eyes toward heaven and my reason returned to me, and I blessed the Most High and praised and honored Him who lives forever;*
>
> *For His dominion is an everlasting dominion, and His kingdom endures from generation to generation. All the inhabitants of the earth are accounted as nothing, but He does according to His will in the host of heaven and among the inhabitants of earth; and no one can ward off His hand or say to Him, "What have you done?"*

> *At that time my reason returned to me. And my majesty and splendor were restored to me for the glory of my kingdom, and my counselors and my nobles began seeking me out; so I was re-established in my sovereignty, and surpassing greatness was added to me.*
>
> *Now I, Nebuchadnezzar, praise, exalt and honor the King of heaven, for all His works are true and His ways just, and He is able to humble those who walk in pride. (Daniel 4: 34-37)*

Nebuchadnezzar finally acknowledged God, and prayed a great prayer of humility and repentance. He recognized that all he had was from God, who "is able to humble those who walk in pride." In the end, God restored him and gave his throne back to him.

Pride Will Hinder Us

Humility before God can lead to His favor, but pride leads to our undoing. A proud man will have problems, difficulty, and hardship because of his pride.

Remember, God wants to use us for His purposes and His glory. He wants to bless us and work through us. Though many are used and blessed greatly, the reality is that having a humble heart before Him is what He desires. Unfortunately, our pride can prevent God from using us. Even more, it will actually cause God to oppose us: *"God resists the proud, but gives grace to the humble"* (James 4:6). Take note of this important point: **God will resist a proud person and will allow circumstances to humble him—for his own good!**

This does not mean that all adversity in our life is due to pride. I fully realize that a humble man, walking with God, can also experience adversity and difficulty. However, whenever we experience adversity, it is a good time to seek God and ask for His wisdom and understanding. When we go to Him with an open heart, He can minister His truth to us. If pride is the problem, He can reveal that to us. If not, He will reveal to us how we are to respond to our adverse circumstances.

Pride brings separation from God and alienates us from others. Our development as believers comes as we interact with God and with people. We are not intended to be islands, or isolated within ourselves. God's plan is for us to be involved with others and have healthy relationships that further our growth.

Pride can thwart these meaningful relationships and thus the growth and positive change He desires. It can keep us from the relationships with those who can speak truth into our lives, and it can keep us from becoming the person God wants us to be.

I have seen these effects in my own life. As a young man, before God revealed this to me, I was on the way to doing severe damage to several of my key relationships. I tended to fight back against my bosses, unwilling to accept their authority as I thought I knew what was best. I was convinced I knew what was needed in my marriage, and would overrule my wife without listening to her.

I did the same in areas of ministry, sure that I was the one that knew what was needed. In order for God to use me as He intended, and to further develop in me what He had for me, He needed to confront my pride.

During this time, I was in fact seeking God and was spiritually motivated. I was trying to be a spiritual man and pleasing to God. Pride was a real blind spot in my life and because I was seeking the Lord He was committed to change me for my good.

God's Spirit wants to reveal pride in us so we can repent of it and walk closer to Him and others.

QUESTIONS FOR REFLECTION AND DISCUSSION

1. How can pride affect:
   a) a man's relationship with God?

   _____
   _____
   _____
   _____

   b) a man's relationships with others?

   _____
   _____
   _____
   _____

   c) God's ability to use a man?

   _____
   _____
   _____
   _____

2. Are there areas in your life where you may be operating in pride? If so, what might they be?

   _____
   _____
   _____
   _____

3. Review the descriptions of a proud man and a humble man. Then, if you are willing, stop and pray now. Ask God to show you any areas of pride that are currently a problem in your life. Write down any impressions that come to you.

_____

_____

_____

_____

TAKE A KNEE

Let's kneel and pray. If you cannot kneel, then kneel in your heart to God. *"Dear Father, I realize that pride can be a destructive force in my life. I also realize it can hurt those I love. Please reveal any pride I need to know about and show me how it has affected those around me, as well as my relationship with You. Forgive me for my pride and change me, renew me, and heal me."*

Chapter 2
BREAKING FREE OF BLIND SPOTS

As I discovered at that work conference, pride can be a part of our lives—obvious to others, and yet completely unnoticed by us!

All of us have pride; we are all guilty. We all need God to reveal to us where pride is negatively affecting our lives and our relationship with Him. This is not a one-time event. Throughout our life, God will be revealing things that He wants to change in us and from which He wants to free us. This process is called sanctification—making our hearts, our thinking, and our character more like Him. By the way, it goes on for our entire life. God is always working on us. So, accept it and embrace it. It is a good thing!

Sanctification, however, can only happen if we are open to it, if we are listening to God, and if are willing to embrace His truth. We can also choose to harden our hearts, refuse to listen, and resist God's workings in our life as Nebuchadnezzar did. The price for hardening our hearts may be high and heartbreaking.

Like Nebuchadnezzar, we can be oblivious to our pride and the effect it has on others. When this happens, we may be suffering from a "blind spot."

Blind Spots

A blind spot is an area where we cannot see a problem in our lives. It can be a behavior, an attitude, an outlook on life, a habit, or a way of treating others. Bad thought patterns or habits we have come to accept can be blind spots. Anger or treating others poorly can be blind spots. A critical spirit or contentious nature can be a blind spot. And pride can be a blind spot. We may not see these areas of shortcoming, may not see them in proper perspective, or may play down their impact. Others, however, often see them clearly.

Chas was enjoying being a part of his church and had just been placed in a position of leadership. The men from the church took a canoe trip where they paired up for the trip down the river. During the trip, Chas and the man in his canoe began to get to know each other and talk about their lives. They had had some limited interaction before this trip, but got to know one another at a deeper level as the hours went by.

Finally, the man shared with Chas that he had been reluctant to get close to him due to Chas' arrogant attitudes. This disturbed Chas; he didn't know how to respond. He didn't realize he came across that way, and now saw it was a problem in his relationship with this man.

He apologized and told the man he didn't want to come across that way. After the canoe trip, Chas regularly thought of the man's comment and began to pray about it. He asked God to give him insight and to change him as needed. God began to give him understanding; as He did and sought God for change, Chas began to change.

An arrogant attitude had been a blind spot for Chas, one that affected his relationships without him knowing it. That's what blind spots do: they cause us to live in a manner that is less than God desires for us.

Detecting and Dealing with a Blind Spot

Sometimes these areas can be very difficult to identify, since they are often such an integral part of who we are. Blind spots can develop from:

- our upbringing, which taught or modeled unbiblical values and philosophies
- unbiblical world or cultural views we have come to accept
- media or entertainment that presents values and philosophies contrary to God's truth
- the influence of friends or peers to think or live contrary to God's truth
- authority figures who have wrongly influenced us
- deception rooted in our hearts; believing things to be true that are unscriptural or false
- a problem in our hearts from allowing attitudes or desires to take root in our hearts that are wrong or harmful to our lives
- coming to wrong conclusions about past circumstances
- bad counsel
- being deeply hurt and our response to it

Sometimes God will open our eyes directly and enable us to recognize an area in which we have been blind. Often, though, he uses others to help us see. God used the men in my company, who were unbelievers, to show me my problem with pride. They were honest, direct, and to the point. It was what I needed to hear. Sometimes, we need others to tell us the truth for our benefit and we have to be willing to hear it.

We all need people we can trust—people who are wise and grounded in God's Word, who can share their insights with us, or speak truth into our lives. Keep in mind that unbelievers can speak truth just as believers can. I personally have had people who are not Christ-followers speak things to me that were truthful and that I needed to hear.

Granted, not everything people share with us will be a blind spot. And, we cannot believe or act on everything people tell us. Some observations might be someone else's opinion, which may be unreliable, unbiblical, or even damaging. So, how do we know when something is a true blind spot versus just a difference of opinion?

I have had people share things with me that after prayer I was convinced was just their opinion. So if we are unsure, we should pray about it. God is our source of wisdom and insight. God knows us as no one else can. He loves us and wants only what is best for us. So, as we pray and seek God about an area of our lives, He will begin to give us insight and truth. If what others are sharing with us is truth and a blind spot, He will be faithful to answer our prayer and give us the understanding we need.

> **Since we are God's creation and His workmanship,**
> **He wants only what is best for us.**
> **He does not want us to be confused,**
> **but conformed to the character of Christ.**

Be relieved; God will not show us all of our shortcomings or blind spots at once. We couldn't take it. He knows the work He is doing in us. However, since it is His purpose to change us according to His will, He delights for us to ask Him to reveal those things that hinder us.

I was driving home one evening and listening to a Christian program on the radio. It occurred to me that often God had to use the 2x4 method of teaching me. That is where I need to be hit over the head with a 2" x 4" board to get my attention! Not literally. But at times it seemed like I learned the hard way.

I didn't want to keep on that path and so I decided to ask God to change my heart and renew my mind as He needed to. I began to pray that for myself daily. I truly believe my heart became more open to Him and He began to change me and reveal things to me I needed to learn. I still pray that today after many years. It has helped my heart to be open to correction and learning.

This does not mean we constantly focus on ourselves and our weaknesses. That can be really hurtful to our lives. Our confidence is in the Lord. He loves us right now, just as we are, shortcomings and all. He can use us and work through us now, shortcomings and all. He in fact wants to use us and work through us while we are in His process. There is no limit to what He can do through us at any time, shortcomings and all.

We should seek Him for direction and follow His leading. If we wait until we are perfect to believe He can use us we will never accomplish anything. None of us are perfect or ever will be in this life. Focusing on our weaknesses or shortcomings will hold us back and keep us from moving forward. The key is that we want to acknowledge God in all we do and give Him the credit for what we accomplish. He's the one who blesses our work.

Responding When God Reveals a Blind Spot

More than once, God has used other people, such as my colleagues, bosses, and my wife, to speak into my life things I needed to hear. There have been times when it was not easy to hear and I resisted in my heart what they said. I couldn't see it, or didn't agree with them at first, and so at times I reacted negatively. Over the years, I have come to understand that seeing these blind spots is a blessing, a true gift. It is not easy, and we must humble ourselves and be willing to listen.

When you know God is showing you a blind spot:

- Be willing to admit an area of shortcoming. Agree with God.
- Ask God to reveal how the area has affected not only your life but also the lives of those around you. Then humbly ask Him for change and healing.
- Find Scripture that deals with this area and begin to think about it (meditate on it) and how it applies to you. Begin to agree with God's Word, pray over it, and ask God to make it real in your life.

When you pray Scripture over your life, it releases God's Spirit to go to work in you. Since you are praying for God's truth to be real in you, and you know that is His will, you can also know that His Spirit will bring it to pass.

- When needed, seek godly counsel and perspective. This can greatly help. Being willing to humble yourself and ask others for counsel may be the key for victory. You are not an island, and God often works through others in the body of Christ.
- If you have offended others or hurt others, ask for their forgiveness.
- Accept God's forgiveness and realize this process is a good thing! It means He loves you and is at work in your life. It's part of His process.

BREAKING FREE OF BLIND SPOTS

We all have blind spots. Sometimes I think I have more than my share. But I realize God wants to develop us all and He is only working to free us of things that can hinder our lives. It does not mean we cannot be used or accomplish the desires God has put in us. God changes us along the way. He wants to bless us and use us. He also wants to continue to make us more like Jesus.*

If I Ask God to Change Me, What Will Happen?

It can be an unsettling thing to ask God to change us in a difficult area such as pride. The devil (speaking of Satan and his forces, who is a very real adversary) will try to convince us that God cannot be trusted. Our own nature (the Bible calls it our "flesh") wants to hang onto itself and resist God's changes. We may like the way we are, or may fear what God will do in order to change us. And, when dealing with an area such as pride, not admitting faults or a need to change are key issues of the problem itself.

Remember, God is committed to develop the character and nature of Christ in us. We can cooperate with this process or resist it. It is human to do both at times. When we resist God, things can become difficult. However, as we seek God and are open to Him to reveal His truth and bring the changes He desires, we see His loving hand at work. The result will be peace and the abundant life He promised.

Jesus said, *"The thief comes only to steal, kill and destroy; I came that they might have life, and have it abundantly"* (John 10:10). The abundant life begins *in* us, and then flows *out* of us. And the apostle Paul wrote, *"Now the Lord is the Spirit; and where the Spirit of the Lord is, there is liberty"* (2 Corinthians 3:17), as well as, *"For*

---

* For more information on breaking free of deep-seated areas that can hinder us, see the study in this series, Overcoming Strongholds.

God has not given us a spirit of fear, but of power and of love and of a sound mind" (2 Timothy 1:7). God wants us to experience His power, His love, and a sound mind. Seek God in this manner and allow Him to change you, heal you, and restore you. Your life will grow richer.

QUESTIONS FOR REFLECTION AND DISCUSSION

1. Have others ever accused you of being a proud person? Consider whether you are open to asking the counsel of others in this area. If so, whom would you ask? If you are married, you should ask your wife.

   _____
   _____
   _____
   _____

2. Are you aware of any "blind spots" about which God may be speaking to you? If so, what are they?

   _____
   _____
   _____
   _____

3. Are you willing to pray and ask God to show you any areas of pride in your life that are a hindrance to you? If so, write out your prayer below.

   _____
   _____

4. Are you able to admit when you are wrong? One indicator is that you are able to list times when you have humbled yourself before others and asked for forgiveness. Think about this and list some of these times here.

5. Please review the list of responses under the section in this chapter "Responding When God Reveals a Blind Spot." Of these, which might you need to do?

TAKE A KNEE

Let's pray. *"Dear Father, I want to be completely open to Your work in me. I want You to have Your will in my life. Even as I pray, begin to move in my life. Your Word says that I can know the truth, and that it will set me free (John 8:32). Make me free with Your truth. I trust You to do only good. Thank You that You love me and want Your best for me."*

Chapter 3

LIVING IN TRUE HUMILITY

In our culture, humility is often thought of as weakness. We are taught to be self-reliant and not show weakness or be vulnerable. Yet the Bible teaches us that humility is good.

When I was a teenager I worked in a delicatessen. The owner, whom we all called "Pop," demonstrated humility to me. This man was not weak, but I was drawn to him because of his ability to demonstrate humility along with his strength and convictions. I felt safe with him and felt I could discuss most anything with him without being condemned or criticized. I also learned a great deal from him. He was always speaking truth and, in his own way, teaching us.

At the same time, those who worked for him felt accepted and valued. He was a unique person whom I have never forgotten. Though he didn't know it, his example taught me much about being a man of courage and conviction, and also about being able to show humility to others at the same time. He spoke the truth without apology, but was patient with me when I didn't always deserve it. He was mentoring me.

The Bible says a lot about these two contrasting attitudes in life—pride and humility. Conquering pride and obtaining humility is of great importance to God. The more we know about a life of true humility, the better able we are to move away from our pride.

Moses is a great example of a man whose life demonstrated humility, yet who was also a man of great conviction and courage. He humbled himself before God continually and sought His will, and at the same time had the courage to lead millions of people and go to war against his enemies when God directed him to do so. Numbers 12:3 tells us of Moses, *"Now the man Moses was very humble, more than all men who were on the face of the earth."*

Most men would think such a man could accomplish little in life, being so humble. But this is a true misunderstanding. Moses boldly spoke to Pharaoh, a ruler of great power, and rebuked him. He stood against thousands of people at times and took a stand for God. He attacked enemies at God's direction and won great battles. But he knew his source of power and success!

Humility does not mean a lack of confidence or a lack of boldness to speak the truth when needed. It does not mean being fearful to move forward to accomplish great things. Rather, it is an understanding of our need of God and our need of His blessing and help to accomplish the things we accomplish. In fact, based on his belief that God is with him and helping him, a humble man might have great confidence that God is working on his behalf to accomplish great things.

The Strength in Humility

Humility is a condition of the heart before God and others. A prideful man focuses his confidence on himself, therefore needing to build himself up. A humble man focuses his confidence in God, and his relationship with Him.

Humility is rooted in trusting God and depending on Him. Humility is also realizing that the flesh (as described in Romans 7) is still a part of us, that we are still prone to sin and live contrary to God's will, and that we have a heart that can be deceived (Jeremiah 17:9). We should have a healthy distrust of ourselves, especially when we leave God out of the equation.

Here's what humility can do for us:

Humility and courage. A truly humble person may show great courage and take on significant tasks; he will have confidence in the outcome, because his trust is not in himself but in God. His actions are based on what he believes God wants or is leading him to do. He also believes God is with him and will help him in his work. He realizes and acknowledges that his talents and abilities are gifts from God. This gives him boldness and courage.

Humility and confidence. A humble person is one who shows compassion to those in need or those going through difficult times; he does not think of himself as better than others. However, he has confidence that he can accomplish any God-given task and believes that God will supernaturally help him as needed. A humble person can have great confidence and boldness, but is not motivated by pride.

Humility and success. A proud person puts his faith in himself and his own abilities. A humble person realizes that God is the source of all gifts, talents, and abilities, and that He expects us to develop them and use them for good.

It is true that many people who are not Christians are highly talented and gifted; they accomplish things with hard work and perseverance, qualities the Bible praises. The question is often asked, "Then why do people who are not Christians and who do not acknowledge God as the source of their gifts and abilities succeed—and sometimes in great ways—while people trying to follow God may have less success?"

But what is success in God's eyes? As believers, we must look beyond the transient success or accomplishments of this life; we must look to the eternal concept of success. Was Jesus successful? Though the world's eyes, many would say no. He didn't build a nice home, raise a wonderful family, or establish a thriving business. But He succeeded in always doing God's will and He accomplished all God purposed for Him. When He said, on the cross, "It is finished," everything God intended for Him to do was done. He accomplished more than any other man who walked the earth. He redeemed mankind back to God.

As men, we need to keep this model of success in mind at all times. God promises to help us in life and in our work. He also promises to help us and bless our finances. But He does not say we will all be rich financially or be famous throughout the world.

A Christian answers to a higher calling and accountability than an unbeliever. He is God's child and one who should want to submit to God's call and purpose for his life. A Christian must answer to God for his attitudes and motivations. For that reason, he cannot compare himself with others when it comes to God's standards.

We cannot allow ourselves to be motivated to be like others, particularly when doing so will take us from God's will or purpose for our lives. That purpose is to conform us to the image and character of His Son: *"For whom He foreknew, He also predestined to be conformed to the image of His Son"* (Romans 8:29).

God desires to develop character in us, part of which is genuine humility. God puts dreams and desires in our hearts that He wants to accomplish through us. We may accomplish great things or live a quiet life. The key is that we have lived for the Lord and accomplished what He desires us to accomplish.

False Humility and Good Pride

I have known a few people who were very proud of their humility. That sounds a bit crazy, but it is true. We can get confused about humility. That's why we need to keep in mind:

Humility is not critical self-condemnation. Humility is not being overly critical of ourselves or condemning ourselves. Honesty, yes. Being willing to admit our mistakes or faults when it is appropriate, yes. But going around with a "woe is me" attitude does not promote humility. We certainly cannot fulfill the biblical commands of having joy, love, faith, hope, peace, and thankfulness if we are moping around.

Humility is a healthy recognition of our shortcomings and humanity, while we rejoice in all God has done for us. Because our hope is in God, we can be positive and joyful. We can still dream big and accomplish all God has for us; we do it with our focus on our relationship with Him.

Realizing that we need God in all areas of life brings humility. We need to recognize and be grateful for His goodness to us. Philippians 4:6-7 speaks of the fruit of thanksgiving. *"Be anxious for nothing, but in everything by prayer and supplication, with thanksgiving, let your requests be made known to God; and the peace of*

God, which surpasses all understanding, will guard your hearts and minds through Christ Jesus." When we are submitted to God, we can experience peace and the other fruits of His Spirit such as being joyful and full of love, having faith and hope, and maintaining a thankful attitude.

Humility is not devaluing yourself. Some people think that, in order to be humble, they have to put themselves down, grovel at others' feet, and count themselves of no value. That is not true humility. In fact, we are of great value to God; we are His children!

Humility is having a mindset that, when appropriate, puts the needs of others before our own. *"Let nothing be done through selfish ambition or conceit,"* Philippians 2:3 says, *"but in lowliness of mind let each esteem others better than himself."* This doesn't mean we do not have value. On the contrary, as I stated, we are of great value to God. But rather than exalting ourselves, we are willing to value others and put their needs first, as Christ did when He came to die for our sins.

This kind of humility comes from a servant's heart, which God greatly values.

We should recognize and use the talents and abilities we have from God. We should also understand the things for which we are well suited. Above all, we should be aware of our need of God and His blessing on our work and activities.

Humility is not a personality trait. Humility is not something in our personalities; as stated, it is a condition of our heart. We all have different personalities. While some are outgoing, others are more quiet and reflective. A dynamic, outgoing person is not necessarily less humble than a quiet one. Regardless of personality, if we put God first and trust Him, we can be positive, cheerful, and be full of hope and faith in God, and also have a humble and submissive heart toward God.

Not all pride is bad pride. Just as we can have false views of humility, we can view pride incorrectly as well. Is all pride bad? Of course not. There is also a healthy expression of pride; this includes "a proper respect for oneself; sense of one's own dignity or worth; self-respect; delight or satisfaction in one's achievements (a job well done)."

You may say of a hard worker, "He takes pride in what he does." A loving father may praise his child by saying, "I am proud of you." This is the good kind of pride; a pride that honors what is good, honorable, loving, and pleasing to God. Even the apostle Paul told the Corinthian church, *"I take great pride in you. I am greatly encouraged; in all our troubles my joy knows no bounds"* (2 Corinthians 7:4).

Humility Takes the Weight Off

Humility is not weakness, it is strength. It is being willing to defer to God and trust Him, and to defer to others when appropriate. Being humble before God brings peace and joy and is life changing.

For years I thought I needed to be perfect. It was difficult for me to receive any type of correction, as it meant that I was not perfect and thus had failed. I was motivated to follow God and be a disciple, and I wanted to be perfect spiritually if possible. I wanted my character to be perfect and wanted to be the perfect guy. I wanted my children to be as perfect as possible—and my wife also.

Spiritual pride is as bad as any form of pride. Not many can measure up and that comes across whether you want it to or not.

My children felt as though they could not live up to my expectations. My wife told me a number of times that she could not live up to my expectations either, and felt like a failure. I guess not many could. I needed to be free of this mindset.

Being a spiritual perfectionist is tough. You want to have all the right answers and be the guy who has it together spiritually. Yet it only leads to a day when you realize it just can't be done. The greatest problem is that you have a standard you cannot live up to, therefore you can never accept yourself. You're set up for a fall.

You have to let yourself off of the hook and let your family off the hook, too. You have to come to the point that's it's okay to admit you failed, or missed the mark, or made a bad decision. Being honest with yourself can really be a relief. Being willing to admit you're not perfect can take great pressure off of yourself.

Discovering God's love, grace, and acceptance is life-changing. I learned this first hand. To know that God loves and accepts us, regardless of our failures and short-comings, is like taking off a giant weight, especially if you think you need to be perfect to be accepted. Diving into the river of God's Spirit and love, on the other hand, is like taking a plunge into an experience from which you never want to recover. Our lives crave and need His love, grace and mercy.

Not only do we need to receive God's grace for our life; we also need to learn to give it to others. Grace is unmerited favor. When we realize God has bestowed His favor on us and we did not earn it or deserve it, it humbles us before Him. It then causes us to extend His grace and favor to others. We become a "grace giver" rather than a condemner. We desperately need God's love and grace, and so does everyone else, whether they realize it or not.

There are times when I am spending time with God that His presence and peace seem to be all around and all over me. I can't get enough of it. It frees me, heals my inner man, and gives me proper perspective. I see life differently and see people differently. It corrects my inner vision. I love it and desperately need it! In light of this perfect love, I am able to admit I am an imperfect being. At the same time, I have more hope than I have ever had because my hope is now in a God who loves me, accepts me, and is faithful to His promises to me.

My focus has changed from trying to live up to a standard I cannot achieve to being able to relax and have a deep inner peace that trusts God for the outcome of all things. My work looks different, my family looks different, my marriage looks different, and my friends look different. They are all, like me, in the process of becoming more like Christ and are loved people. He accepts and loves us just as we are!

Do you want inner peace? Do you want to be free of needing to be perfect to be accepted? Do you want to experience God's love and His peace. Take the plunge! Go after God. Admit your need to Him and ask Him to reveal His love and peace to you. It will change your life. You won't have to perform to be loved. He has wisdom, knowledge, direction, and revelation saved up for you and is ready to give it as you go to Him and ask Him for it. It's a free gift. He wants to love on you and bless your life.

Revelation 21:6-7 says, *"I will give of the fountain of the water of life freely to him who thirsts. He who overcomes shall inherit all things, and I will be his God and he shall be My son."* If you are His child, this promise if for you! If you are not His child, ask Him to come into your life and be your Savior and this promise becomes yours. Are you thirsty? Take a drink of Him. His is ready to quench your thirst. God's love will transform you and give you true humility and grace.

QUESTIONS FOR REFLECTION AND DISCUSSION

1. To what extent are you trying to earn God's (or others') favor by your own accomplishments and merit? Only you and God know for sure. Write your thoughts below.

2. Have you known (or known of) a man who was both humble and bold? How did he display these traits?

3. How would you define false humility?

4. How would greater freedom to be flawed and open before the Lord change the way you approach your relationships (e.g., with your wife and children, or in your work/ministry/community)?

_____

_____

_____

TAKE A KNEE

Let's pray: *"Dear Father, I want to yield my heart and life to You. I choose to trust You and desire You to work in my life to make me more like Christ. I believe that You love me and want only good in my life. So I ask You now to take delight in me and free me of anything that is hindering me. I accept that I am complete in You and desire Your complete nature, which is resident in me by Your Spirit, to flow out more fully. Thank You for Your love, grace and mercy in my life."*

A FINAL WORD

Pride is a difficult issue because in addressing it, we are dealing with the heart and possibly issues of the past. It can involve our upbringing, our motivations, and our core values. We are also dealing with what the Bible calls the "Flesh", or the part of us that wants to have our own way instead of following God and submitting to Him. Regardless, this is an area in which God desires to change us and free us as He changes us into the image of His Son. That unique combination of being humble, as well as bold and courageous, is something only God can work in us.

Pride says, "What do I want?"

Humility says, "What is best? What is the right thing to do? What does God want?" Pride says, "I have the answers.

Humility says, "God has the answers, and I need to seek Him for wisdom, guidance and direction."

Being open to God's Spirit, believing He truly loves us, and trusting Him to do only good in our lives is a key to letting go in this area and letting God work in us. It will bring greater peace, a richer relationship with God and others, and teach us to trust Him in a greater way.

Are you willing to step out in faith in this issue and allow God to work in your life? It will never be the same. This is a good thing! Take the plunge!

ABOUT THE AUTHOR

Lou Turner wrote *Living Life God's Way* out of his passion for men to discover God, and to get to know Him and what He has for them. This 13-book men's discipleship series is the culmination of Lou's own journey—a life of seeking God, studying His Word, memorizing Scripture and meditating on it, and practical experience with family, community, marketplace work, and Christian ministry. It also comes, by Lou's own admission, from life experiences of both successes and mistakes, as a result of both good and bad decisions.

Lou has headed ministries, written and taught workshops, classes, and seminars, and discipled dozens of men. Now, he has put into print the things he has learned to help other men along their path and journey.

Most of Lou's growing up years were spent in Detroit and its suburbs, where he was raised in a pastor's home. Following his graduation from university with a Bachelor of Science in Business Administration, Lou and his wife planted and pastored a church for three years. After that time, he felt the strong call of God to return to business.

Over the years, Lou has served in numerous senior executive positions with national and international companies in the real estate and oil and gas industries. As of this writing, Lou is still active in business with his own home building company. He has

ABOUT THE AUTHOR

been married to his wife Joan since they were 20. They have three children and 10 grandchildren and make their home in Phoenix, Arizona.

www.ingramcontent.com/pod-product-compliance
Lightning Source LLC
Chambersburg PA
CBHW021124080526
44587CB00010B/636